Foreword

Are you looking to get or have decided on making a Newfoundland puppy part of your family and need a detailed resource to help you raise your new puppy to be a healthy Gentle Giant, then look now further!

Newfoundland dogs are undeniably gentle giants and making the decision to bring one into your life will give you more joy and love than any canine can offer! There is no shortage of loyalty and loving looks with a Newfoundlander.

With so much information out there- where do you find a book dedicated to such an amazing breed? That is what you will find with "Beginners Guide to Raising a Newfoundland Puppy" !

Whats included in this breed dedicated book?

- History and knowledge of this incredible breed
- Items needed to keep them happy and healthy
- Exploring simple training and safety practices
- Understanding how to care for their double coats
- Different stages of their lives
- Health issues to be aware of

This book gives you a simplified breakdown in one resourceful handy location to help you raise your new Newfoundland Puppy and give them a great life.

If you are looking to raise a Newfoundland Gentle Giant, than don't do it alone, join me and I'll see you on the inside!

Chapter 1

Introduction:

In the heartwarming realm of canine companionship, few breeds embody the spirit of devotion and gentleness quite like the Newfoundland. This comprehensive guide serves as an educational tool for you as you embarking on the journey of raising your magnificent gentle giant.

Welcome to a world where the love and loyalty of a Newfoundland will enrich your life in ways that are unimaginable. From their origins as hardworking water rescue dogs to becoming beloved family members, Newfoundlands captivate hearts with their majestic presence and warm, nurturing nature.

Welcome to the World of Newfoundland Dogs

In the ever evolving world of canine companionship, there exists a breed that stands out not only for its impressive size but also for its gentle nature and unwavering loyalty—the Newfoundland dog. Welcome to the world of Newfoundland companionship, where the bond between human and gentle giant surpass your standard furry companion relationship.

Overview of the Newfoundland Breed

As you embark on this extraordinary journey of raising a Newfoundland, it's essential to understand the unique characteristics that define this majestic breed. Originating from the rugged coasts of Newfoundland Canada, these dogs were initially bred to assist fishermen in their demanding tasks. With a strong body structure, webbed feet, and a thick water-resistant double coat, Newfoundlands proved to be an invaluable companion for fisherman and water rescue missions.

Chapter 2

Understanding the Newfoundland Breed: History, Origin, and Breed Standards

These gentle giants have unique needs, and ensuring a harmonious match requires considering various factors. Before delving into the practical aspects of raising a Newfoundland, it's crucial to appreciate and understand the breed's history, characteristics, and unique needs. Understanding their origins as working dogs provides valuable insights into their intelligence, train-ability, and natural instincts.

The Breed's Roots as Working Dogs

To truly appreciate the Newfoundland breed, it's essential to delve into its rich history as a working dog. Originating from the rugged island of Newfoundland Canada, these dogs were integral to the lives of 18th-century fishermen. They were initially bred for utilitarian purposes. Their primary role involved aiding fishermen in the demanding tasks of hauling nets, retrieving fishing gear, and even rescuing people at risk of drowning. The Newfoundland's exceptional swimming ability, strength, and endurance in harsh, cold waters quickly made them indispensable working companions along the Atlantic coast.

Working Instincts

Rooted in their history as working dogs, Newfoundlands retain certain instincts that can be seen in their behavior today. They are natural swimmers and often exhibit a strong affinity for water. Their loyalty and protective nature make them excellent watchdogs, while their strength can be harnessed in various working roles.

Traits that Make Newfoundlands Exceptional

The Newfoundland's working heritage has bestowed upon them a set of exceptional traits that extend beyond their original purpose. Renowned for their gentle and kind nature, Newfoundlands exhibit an unparalleled devotion to their human companions. Their intelligence, coupled with a calm demeanor, makes them versatile and adaptable, excelling in various roles beyond their historical duties. These qualities have endeared them to families worldwide, contributing to their reputation as loyal, gentle giants.

Newfoundlands are a testament to the harmonious blend of strength and gentleness. Their intelligence, paired with an eagerness to please, makes them highly trainable. Their history as working dogs has given them a strong work ethic and a natural instinct to protect those they consider part of their family.

The gentle temperament of Newfoundlands extends beyond their familial bonds; they are known for their calm disposition in various situations, making them excellent therapy dogs. Their innate sense of responsibility and loyalty means that they not only make great family pets but also compassionate service animals.

Size and Structure Considerations

Beyond their utilitarian roots, as cherished members of households worldwide, Newfoundlands bring their remarkable traits—gentleness, intelligence, affectionate nature, patience, and a protective instinct—to the forefront of family life. Newfoundlands should display grace and athleticism, moving with a certain degree of fluidity. The breed standards emphasize a powerful yet agile physique, ensuring that Newfoundlands maintain both strength and agility.They are notably large dogs, with males typically weighing between 130 to 150 pounds and females between 100 to 120 pounds, their size might be intimidating at first glance, but these gentle giants have hearts as large as their frames.

Newfoundlands are known for their distinctive appearance, characterized by a broad head, dark eyes with a gentle expression that reflects their warm-hearted disposition. The breed's signature coat comes in various colors, including black, brown, gray, and Landseer, which is a striking combination of white with black markings.

The Newfoundland's Gentle Temperament

One of the most endearing qualities of Newfoundland dogs is their compassionate temperament. Renowned for their calm demeanor, they exude a natural kindness that endears them to individuals of all ages. Their patience and tolerance makes them excellent companions for families, especially those with children. Despite their imposing size, Newfoundlands are known for being gentle giants, often described as "nannies" due to their protective and nurturing instincts, making them a top choice for families with children.

These dogs thrive on human companionship and are known to form strong bonds with their owners. Whether you're seeking a loyal friend for your outdoor adventures or a gentle giant to share quiet moments snuggling while reading a good book, the Newfoundland's adaptable nature makes them a perfect fit for various lifestyles.

Intelligence and Train-ability

Newfoundlands are intelligent dogs, quick learners, and eager to please their owners. This, coupled with their calm nature, makes them relatively easy to train. They respond well to positive reinforcement techniques and thrive on the bond formed through consistent, gentle guidance. Their train-ability is an asset, especially considering their substantial size.

Physical Characteristics

Newfoundlands are large, robust dogs with a powerful build. They possess a distinctive double coat that consists of a water-resistant outer layer and a dense, insulating undercoat. Their webbed feet, a nod to their aquatic heritage, aid in efficient swimming.

Recognized Coat Colors and Markings

The Newfoundland breed boasts a stunning range of coat colors and markings, each contributing to their unique charm. Recognized colors include solid black, brown, gray, and the distinctive Landseer, characterized by a white coat with black markings, often showcases a white body with a black head, along with black markings on the body. While black is the most common color, each variation is acknowledged and celebrated within breed standards and help create a diverse Newfoundland breed community.

- **Black:** The classic black Newfoundland is perhaps the most iconic, exuding an air of dignity and strength. Their solid black coats are sleek and impressive.
- **Brown**: The warm, chocolate hues of the brown Newfoundland are equally captivating. This variation adds a touch of earthy charm to the breed, emphasizing their approachable nature.
- **Gray**: A regal shade, the gray Newfoundland showcases a distinguished mix of tones, creating a striking and majestic appearance.
- **Landseer**: Named after the famous artist Edwin Landseer, Landseer Newfoundlands are characterized by a predominantly white coat with distinct black markings. This variation adds a touch of artistry to the breed, making Landseers particularly captivating.

Understanding these coat variations not only allows for a deeper appreciation of the Newfoundland's aesthetics but also aids in recognizing the breed's genetic diversity.

As you navigate the chapters ahead, you'll gain insights into effective training methods, healthcare practices, and the art of fostering a deep, meaningful connection with your Newfoundland companion. The journey of raising a Newfoundland is not just about caring for a pet; it's a shared adventure, a harmonious companionship between human and dog.

In the chapters to come, we'll explore the importance of grooming, training, nutrition, and healthcare specific to Newfoundland dogs. As you embark on this enriching journey, remember that you're not merely raising a pet; you're cultivating a lifelong bond with a gentle giant—a Newfoundland companion that will undoubtedly leave paw prints on your heart.

Choosing, Preparing, and Welcoming Your Gentle Giant

Choosing to welcome a Newfoundland into your home is a commitment to joy, companionship, and responsible pet ownership. This chapter serves as your compass in navigating the process of selecting the right Newfoundland puppy for you, considering factors such as your lifestyle, living space, and the reputation of breeders or rescue organizations. Dive into the essentials of puppy-proofing your home, ensuring a safe and welcoming environment for your furry family member. Discover the necessary supplies, from cozy bedding to the art of crate training, that will set the stage for a less stressful integration of your Newfoundland into your household.

As we embark on this guide together, brace yourself for an adventure filled with love, laughter, and the extraordinary companionship that only a Newfoundland can provide. From puppy hood to the golden years, each chapter unfolds a new layer of the Newfoundland experience, equipping you with the knowledge and insights essential to raising your gentle giant with confidence and care.

Choosing the Right Newfoundland

Evaluating Your Lifestyle and Space

The decision to bring a Newfoundland puppy into your life is both exciting and significant. Before diving into the world of fluffy paws and wagging tails, it's crucial to evaluate your lifestyle and living space. Newfoundlands are known for their substantial size and gentle temperament, making them a great fit for various environments, but a successful match depends on thoughtful consideration.

Consider your daily routine, activity level, and the amount of time you can dedicate to your canine companion. Newfoundlands thrive on human interaction and require moderate exercise, so if you lead an active lifestyle and have ample time for walks and play, a Newfoundland could be an ideal addition.

Space is another crucial factor. While Newfoundlands adapt well to apartment living if given sufficient exercise, a house with a yard provides them with more room to roam. Their large size means they appreciate having space to stretch out, both indoors and outdoors.

Finding Reputable Breeders or Rescue Organizations

Once you've assessed your lifestyle and living arrangements, the next step is to find the right source for your Newfoundland puppy. Reputable breeders and rescue organizations play a vital role in ensuring the health and well-being of your future furry friend.

Ensure that you source your Newfoundland puppy from a reputable breeder or rescue organization that you have researched and or gathered recommendations for. Responsible breeders prioritize the health, temperament, and ethical treatment of their dogs. Thoroughly research breeders, seeking those with positive reviews, adherence to breed standards, and a commitment to the overall well-being of the Newfoundland breed, ask for references, and visit their facilities if possible. Ethical breeders are dedicated to the Newfoundland breed, conducting health screenings for genetic conditions and providing a loving environment for the puppies.

If opting for adoption, a reputable rescue organizations can provide valuable information about a puppy's background, health, and behavioral traits. Always consider reputable rescue organizations that specialize in Newfoundlands. Adopting a Newfoundland puppy can be a rewarding experience, offering a second chance to a dog in need. These organizations often assess the temperament of the dogs in their care and provide valuable information about the dog's history and needs.

Adapting for a Large Breed

Newfoundland puppies, with their rapid growth and exuberance, require a home environment adapted to their size. Identify and address potential hazards, securing areas where your puppy will roam. Remove any small objects, electrical cords, or low-lying items that could pose risks. Consider installing baby gates to limit access to certain areas, ensuring your Newfoundland's safety as they explore their new surroundings. Being proactive in creating a secure space for your puppy helps foster a smooth transition into your home.

Essential Supplies for a Newfoundland Puppy

Newfoundland puppies, while undeniably adorable, come with a considerable size that demands careful consideration when preparing your home. Puppy-proofing is not just about protecting your belongings; it's about creating a safe and comfortable environment for your growing gentle giant.

Welcoming a Newfoundland puppy involves gathering essential supplies tailored to their specific needs. Invest in a spacious and comfortable bed, taking into account the breed's size and potential growth. Sturdy food and water bowls designed for large breeds, like raised food stands support healthy eating habits. Choose toys that cater to their size and chewing tendencies, promoting mental stimulation and play.

Additionally, acquire a sizable crate with a removable divider suitable for training and providing a secure retreat for your puppy when needed.

Secure Your Space

Ensure that your living space is secure and free of potential hazards. Newfoundlands are known to be curious and may explore every nook and cranny. Install baby gates to limit access to certain areas and create designated safe zones for your puppy.

Invest in Sturdy Furniture

Newfoundlands grow rapidly, and what may seem like a small puppy today can become a hefty dog tomorrow. Invest in sturdy, large-sized furniture that can withstand the weight and size of a fully grown Newfoundland. This includes a sturdy bed, as Newfoundlands appreciate having their own comfortable space.

Pup-Proof Your Garden

If you have an outdoor space, ensure it's securely fenced to prevent adventurous escapades. Newfoundlands are excellent swimmers, but not all bodies of water are safe for them. Pools and ponds should be securely covered or fenced off to avoid any accidents.

Consider Your Flooring

Newfoundlands are known for their love of water, and that often means wet, muddy paws. Choose flooring that is easy to clean and resistant to moisture. This is especially important in areas where your puppy is likely to spend a significant amount of time.

In conclusion, preparing for your Newfoundland puppy involves a thoughtful evaluation of your lifestyle, finding a reputable source, and creating a safe haven for your growing companion. By taking these steps, you set the stage for a harmonious and fulfilling relationship with your gentle giant in the making. In the following chapters, we'll delve into the early days of bringing your Newfoundland puppy home and the essential aspects of their care and training.

Interactive Toys and Mental Stimulation

Keep your Newfoundland puppy mentally stimulated with interactive, size appropriate toys and puzzles. These not only provide entertainment but also help channel their intelligence and energy in positive ways.

High-Quality Puppy Food

Choose a high-quality puppy food designed for large breeds. Consult with your veterinarian to determine the appropriate feeding schedule and portion sizes.

Grooming Supplies

Newfoundland puppies have a thick, water-resistant double coat. Regular grooming is essential to prevent matting. Have the necessary grooming supplies, including a brush, comb, and nail clippers.

Collar and Leash

Introduce your puppy to a collar and leash early on. Opt for adjustable, comfortable options that can accommodate their growing size.

By carefully selecting your Newfoundland, puppy-proofing your home, and gathering essential supplies, you're laying the foundation for a positive and enriching experience for both you and your newfound furry friend. In the upcoming chapters, we'll explore the initial days of bringing your Newfoundland puppy home and delve into essential aspects of their care and training.

Growth Stages

Newfoundland puppies undergo rapid growth during their first year, and being mindful of this process is essential. From the initial adorable fluff ball to the imposing adult, your puppy will experience significant changes. Providing a balanced diet designed for large breeds is crucial during this growth period to support healthy bone development and overall well-being.

Tracking your puppy's weight and consulting with your veterinarian will help ensure they are on the right growth path. While it's tempting to indulge in treats, maintaining a healthy weight is vital to prevent joint issues and other health concerns associated with excess weight on their frame.

Adult Size and Weight

Newfoundlands are known for their considerable size, with males typically weighing between 130 to 150 pounds and females ranging from 100 to 120 pounds. While their sheer mass might be intimidating, their gentle temperament and easygoing nature make them approachable companions. As your puppy transforms into a full-grown Newfoundland, be prepared for the majestic presence they'll command.

Structural Considerations

Unique Features

Newfoundlands possess distinctive physical attributes that contribute to their charm and functionality. Their large, expressive heads, adorned with soulful eyes characterized by a gentle expression that mirrors their affectionate nature and well-set ears, create a gentle and kind expression.

The breed's broad chest and muscular build reflect their strength and endurance, traits deeply rooted in their history as working dogs.

The Water-Resistant Coat

One of the most iconic features of Newfoundlands is their double coat. This dense, water-resistant fur serves both functional and aesthetic purposes. Regular grooming is essential to maintain the coat's health and protect it from matting.

Webbed Feet

Newfoundlands boast webbed feet, a testament to their exceptional swimming abilities. Whether they're splashing around for recreation or performing water rescues, their webbed paws propel them through the water with grace and efficiency.

Grooming Practices

Regular grooming is a fundamental aspect of caring for your Newfoundland's distinctive coat. Brushing should be a consistent routine to prevent mats and tangles, which left unattended can turn into health issues. Additionally, pay attention to their ears, paws, and tail, ensuring these areas remain clean and free from debris.

Exercise and Joint Health

While Newfoundlands are not overly energetic, regular exercise is crucial to maintaining their overall health. Low-impact activities like swimming, short walks, and playtime in a secure area are ideal. Be mindful of their joints, as their size makes them susceptible to certain orthopedic issues. Using a ramp for loading and unloading from your vehicle and reducing stairs is recommended. Consult with your veterinarian to establish an exercise routine tailored to your Newfoundland's needs.

Understanding the size and structure considerations unique to Newfoundlands empowers you as a caregiver to provide the necessary care and attention. In the upcoming chapters, we will explore the specifics of grooming, exercise, and healthcare practices to ensure your gentle giant thrives in every aspect of their well-being.

Embarking on the journey of raising a Newfoundland puppy requires careful consideration and preparation. By aligning your lifestyle, choosing reliable sources, and creating a safe and welcoming environment, you set the stage for a positive and fulfilling experience as you introduce your gentle giant into your home and heart.

Chapter 5

Bringing Your Newfoundland Puppy Home: A Warm Welcome for Your New Companion

Introduction to the New Environment

The initial days and nights with your Newfoundland puppy are crucial for establishing a sense of security. Introduce your puppy to their new surroundings gradually, allowing them to explore different areas of your home while providing a safe space where they can retreat if needed. Create a cozy spot with their bed and familiar items, offering a comforting environment as they acclimate to their new home.

Safe Space

Designate a safe and comfortable area for your puppy to acclimate to their new surroundings. This space should include their bed, food and water bowls, and a few familiar toys. Gradually introduce them to different areas of your home as to not overwhelm them.

Patience and Calmness

Understand that the transition can be overwhelming for your puppy. Approach the introduction with patience and calmness. Spend time sitting with them in their safe space to build trust.

Establishing Routines for Feeding, Potty Breaks, and Playtime

Consistency is key in the early days. Establish clear routines for feeding, potty breaks, and playtime. Set a regular feeding schedule to promote healthy eating habits and predictability. Take your Newfoundland puppy outside for potty breaks at consistent intervals, reinforcing positive behavior with praise. Incorporate playtime to strengthen the bond and provide physical and mental stimulation. A well-structured routine builds a foundation of security and trust.

Feeding Schedule

Determine a regular feeding schedule and stick to it. High-quality puppy food for large breeds is essential for their growth. Monitor their weight and adjust portions as needed.

Potty Breaks

Take your puppy outside frequently for potty breaks, especially after meals and playtime. Positive reinforcement for successful outdoor potty breaks helps them associate the right behavior with positive outcomes.

Playtime and Exercise

Engage in short, gentle play sessions away from feeding time to allow your puppy to burn off energy on a calm stomach. Newfoundlands may not have excessive energy, but regular playtime is essential for their physical and mental well-being.

Building Trust with Your Newfoundland

Building trust is fundamental to a strong bond with your Newfoundland puppy. Spend quality time together, engaging in gentle activities that allow your puppy to become familiar with your touch and voice. Use positive reinforcement techniques during training, rewarding good behavior with treats and affection. Approach interactions with patience and understanding, allowing your Newfoundland to feel secure in your presence. During the early days, focus on creating positive associations with your presence.

Gentle Interactions

Approach your puppy with gentleness. Use soft, reassuring tones and avoid sudden movements. Allow them to come to you at their own pace, fostering trust and comfort. This is a big thing to teach your children.

Positive Reinforcement

Use positive reinforcement techniques during training and everyday interactions. Reward good behavior with treats, praise, and affection. This builds a positive association with following commands.

Positive Interactions with Family Members and Other Pets

Welcoming a Newfoundland puppy into your home is a joyous occasion filled with discovery and bonding. By carefully introducing them to their new environment and establishing routines, providing a foundation of comfort and build their trust.

Gradual Introductions

Monitor interactions to ensure everyone is comfortable. Socialization is a vital aspect of your Newfoundland puppy's development. Encourage positive interactions with family members by involving them in playtime, feeding, and short training sessions. Supervise introductions to other pets and always supervise interactions between your Newfoundland puppy and younger family members, ensuring a calm and controlled environment. Gradually expose your puppy to various sights, sounds, and experiences to foster a well-adjusted and socially adept companion. Positive socialization experiences contribute to a well-rounded and confident Newfoundland.

Socialization Opportunities

Provide positive socialization experiences by exposing your puppy to various environments, people, and other animals. This helps them develop into well-adjusted adults with positive behavior.

Puppy Training Classes

Consider enrolling in puppy training classes. These not only provide essential obedience training but also offer opportunities for positive socialization with other puppies.

As you navigate the initial days of bringing your Newfoundland puppy home, remember that patience, consistency, and positive reinforcement are key. The strong foundation you establish during these early moments will set the stage for a loving and enduring bond. In the chapters to come, we'll explore the specific aspects of grooming, training, and healthcare tailored to the needs of your growing Newfoundland companion.

Chapter 6

Basic Training for Newfoundland Puppies: Fostering Good Behavior with Positive Reinforcement

Reward-Based Training Methods

Newfoundland puppies respond exceptionally well to positive reinforcement. Use treats, praise, and affection as rewards for good behavior. When your puppy successfully follows a command or exhibits desirable conduct, immediately reward them. Consistency in rewarding positive actions helps reinforce the desired behavior, making the learning experience enjoyable for your New

Positive reinforcement is the cornerstone of effective training for Newfoundland puppies. This approach focuses on rewarding desirable behavior, creating a positive association between the behavior and the reward.

Treats and Praise

Use high-value treats to reward your puppy when they exhibit the desired behavior. You may need to try different options until you find the ones they respond to best. Coupled with verbal praise and affectionate gestures, treats become powerful motivators.

Timing is Crucial

Timing is key in positive reinforcement. Deliver the reward immediately after the desired behavior occurs. This helps your puppy associate the reward with the specific action.

Consistency and Patience in Commands

Consistency and patience form the bedrock of successful training. Newfoundland puppies, known for their intelligence, respond well to routines and clear expectations.

Consistent Commands

Use consistent commands for specific behaviors. Whether it's "sit," "stay," or any other command, maintaining uniformity helps your puppy understand and respond appropriately.

Consistency is the cornerstone of effective training. Use the same commands consistently for specific actions, such as "sit," "stay," or "come." Be patient and understanding, recognizing that puppies may take time to grasp new concepts. Maintain a calm and positive demeanor during training sessions, creating an environment where your Newfoundland feels encouraged to learn and respond.

Patience in Learning

Puppies are like sponges, absorbing information at their own pace. Exercise patience as your Newfoundland learns new commands. Repetition and positive reinforcement will help solidify their understanding.

Sit, Stay, Come, and Leave It

Sit: Teach your Newfoundland puppy to sit on command by holding a treat above their head. As they follow the treat, gently guide their back end down.Reward them immediately, reinforcing the association between the command and the action, and repeat the process consistently.

Stay: Teaching "stay" is crucial for safety. Encourage the "stay" command by having your puppy sit, then take a step back. Use an open hand, signaling them to stay. Gradually increase the distance and duration as your puppy becomes more comfortable with the command.

Come: A reliable recall is essential for off-leash activities. Teach your Newfoundland to come when called by using a cheerful tone and offering a treat. Begin in a controlled environment, gradually adding distractions. Rewarding their response reinforces the importance of coming when called.

Leave It: This command is vital for a puppy's safety and preventing undesirable behaviors . Hold a treat in your closed hand and present it to your puppy. When they show interest, say "leave it" and wait for them to lose interest. Reward them with a different treat, reinforcing that "leave it" leads to a better reward.

Introduce the Leash

Start by allowing your Newfoundland puppy to get used to the feel of the leash. Attach the leash and let them explore while supervised indoors. Gradually progress to short, positive outdoor walks, associating it with positive experiences. Use treats and praise as they become accustomed to the leash.

Walking Etiquette

Teach your puppy to walk beside you without pulling by using treats and positive reinforcement. When they walk without pulling, reward them. If they start to pull, stop walking and wait for them to return to your side before continuing. Consistent reinforcement creates a positive association with loose-leash walking.

Positive Exposure

Expose your puppy to various environments during walks. This helps them become comfortable with different sights, sounds, and smells, contributing to their socialization.

Training your Newfoundland puppy is a rewarding journey that strengthens the bond between you and your furry companion. Incorporating these positive reinforcement techniques and essential commands into your Newfoundland puppy's training regimen sets the stage for a well-behaved and socially adept companion. Consistency, patience, and positive interactions during training create a positive learning experience, fostering a strong bond with your gentle giant. In the upcoming chapters, we'll explore advanced training techniques and specific care routines tailored to your growing Newfoundland.

Brushing and Maintaining a Healthy Coat

Newfoundland dogs are known for their luxurious double coat, which requires regular brushing to keep it healthy and free from mats. Use a slicker brush and comb to gently remove loose hair, tangles, and debris. Aim for at least two to three brushing sessions per week to prevent matting and distribute natural oils, promoting a shiny and healthy coat.

Regular Brushing

Embrace the ritual of brushing your Newfoundland's coat at least two to three times a week. This not only prevents matting but also serves as a bonding experience. Utilize a slicker brush or comb designed for double-coated breeds, reaching down to the undercoat for a thorough grooming session.

Focus on the Undercoat

The undercoat, being dense and prone to matting, requires special care. Pay attention to this layer during brushing to prevent tangles and mat formation. A well-maintained undercoat contributes to the overall health of the skin and coat.

Coat Health Products

Consider incorporating coat health products, such as conditioners and detanglers, into your grooming routine. These products help keep the coat silky and manageable, reducing the risk of mats.

Dealing with Shedding and Seasonal Coat Changes

Newfoundlands undergo shedding, especially during seasonal changes, also known as blowing their coat. Increase brushing frequency during shedding seasons to manage loose hair and reduce the amount of fur around the home. While shedding is a natural process, a consistent grooming routine helps minimize loose hair and keeps your Newfoundland's coat in top condition.

Shedding Control

Manage shedding by incorporating a high-quality de-shedding tool into your grooming arsenal. This tool proves especially effective during shedding seasons, reducing the amount of loose hair in your home.

Seasonal Coat Changes

Acknowledge the seasonal changes in your Newfoundland's coat. Increase the frequency of brushing during warmer months to help them shed their undercoat, promoting comfort and an overall healthier coat.

Nail Trimming, Ear Cleaning, and Dental Care

In addition to coat care, attend to your Newfoundland's nails, ears, and teeth to ensure their overall well-being.

- **Nail Trimming**: Regular nail trims are essential to maintain health, prevent discomfort and potential injury. Aim for a trim every 3-4 weeks. Introduce your Newfoundland puppy to nail trimming gradually, associating the process with positive experiences and treats. Use a quality nail clipper or grinder, ensuring not to cut into the quick. If unsure, seek guidance from your veterinarian or a professional groomer.
- **Ear Cleaning**: Newfoundland ears, especially those with the Landseer coat, can be susceptible to moisture-related issues. Routinely inspect your Newfoundland's ears regularly for dirt, wax, or signs of infection. Use a damp cotton ball or a veterinarian-recommended ear cleaner to gently wipe the ear's interior. Avoid inserting anything into the ear canal. Consistent ear cleaning helps prevent infections and ensures optimal ear health.
- **Dental Care:** Prioritize dental health by introducing a regular teeth brushing routine. Dental hygiene is crucial for your Newfoundland's overall well-being. Establish a routine of brushing their teeth at least two to three times a week using a dog-friendly toothbrush and toothpaste. Dental chews or toys designed to promote oral health can also be incorporated into their routine. Regular dental care aids in preventing plaque buildup and maintaining healthy gums.

Caring for the grooming needs of your Newfoundland is a rewarding aspect of responsible pet ownership. Establishing a consistent grooming routine not only enhances their majestic appearance but also contributes to their overall comfort and well-being. Regular check-ups with a veterinarian ensure that your gentle giant receives comprehensive care, promoting a lifetime of health and happiness.

Schedule routine veterinary check-ups to monitor your Newfoundland's health and address any grooming or care concerns. Veterinarians can provide professional guidance on grooming practices, dental care, and overall well-being. These regular visits are crucial for identifying and addressing potential health issues early on, ensuring your Newfoundland enjoys a happy and healthy life.

Comprehensive Health Assessment

Schedule routine veterinary check-ups to assess your Newfoundland's overall health. These visits provide an opportunity for your vet to detect potential issues early on, ensuring prompt intervention if needed.

Vaccinations and Preventive Care

Stay diligent with vaccinations and preventive care recommended by your veterinarian. Maintain a schedule for flea and tick prevention, heart-worm medication, and other preventive measures tailored to your Newfoundland's specific needs.

By incorporating detailed care into your Newfoundland's grooming routine and consistently prioritizing their overall health, you lay the foundation for a happy, healthy, and well-groomed companion. This commitment not only enhances their physical well-being but also strengthens the unique bond between you and your gentle giant. In the subsequent chapters, we will delve into advanced training techniques and explore specific aspects of nutrition and healthcare tailored to your growing Newfoundland.

Chapter 8

Nutrition and Health for Your Newfoundland: Nourishing Their Well-Being and Addressing Health Concerns

Newfoundlands, with their robust stature and gentle demeanor, require meticulous attention to their nutrition and health. This chapter delves into the essential aspects of proper nutrition for Newfoundland puppies and addresses common health concerns, including the crucial concept of growing slowly to prevent joint issues as they age.

Proper Nutrition for Newfoundland Puppies -Choosing the Right Food and Feeding Schedule

Quality Puppy Food

Opt for high-quality puppy food specifically formulated for large breeds. Ensure the food meets the nutritional requirements outlined by reputable organizations. Look for ingredients such as meat, whole grains, and essential vitamins and minerals.

Feeding Schedule

Establish a consistent feeding schedule for your Newfoundland puppy, typically involving three meals a day during puppy hood. This routine provides a steady stream of nutrients, accommodating their growing bodies and preventing digestive issues. As they mature, transition to two meals a day. Consult your veterinarian for specific guidelines based on your puppy's age, weight, and health.

Monitoring Growth and Weight

Healthy Growth

Newfoundland puppies grow rapidly, and it's crucial to monitor their growth to ensure it's steady and appropriate for their breed. Avoid overfeeding, as excessive weight gain can lead to developmental issues. Regularly consult your veterinarian to adjust the feeding plan as your puppy matures. Embrace the principle of growing slow to mitigate the risk of joint issues as your Newfoundland puppy ages. Rapid growth can contribute to orthopedic problems, such as hip and elbow dysplasia. Resist the temptation to overfeed, as controlled growth is paramount for their well-being.

Regular Weigh-Ins

Regularly monitor your Newfoundland puppy's weight to ensure they are growing at a healthy rate. Sudden weight fluctuations can indicate underlying health issues or dietary imbalances. Use this information to make informed adjustments to their diet as needed.

Adjusting Portions

Adjust food portions based on your puppy's age, activity level, and overall health. Newfoundland puppies should maintain a lean body condition to reduce stress on developing joints, mitigating the risk of orthopedic issues.

Nutritional Supplements

Consult with your veterinarian before introducing any nutritional supplements. While a balanced diet typically meets your puppy's needs, certain situations may warrant additional supplements, such as omega-3 fatty acids for coat health.

Growing Slow for Joint Health

Prioritize controlled and steady growth for your Newfoundland puppy. Growing too quickly can strain developing joints, leading to potential joint issues as they age. Consult with your veterinarian to determine the appropriate growth rate and nutritional approach to support optimal joint health

Nutrition for Heart Health

Incorporate heart-healthy nutrients into your Newfoundland's diet, such as omega-3 fatty acids. These can be obtained from fish oil supplements or foods rich in these essential fatty acids.

Common Health Concerns in Newfoundlands

Hip and Elbow Dysplasia

Regular Exercise

Maintain a balanced exercise routine that supports muscle development without putting excessive strain on the joints. Controlled, low-impact exercises are beneficial for overall joint health.

Proper Nutrition

A well-balanced diet, including joint supplements recommended by your veterinarian, can contribute to joint health. Monitor your Newfoundland's weight to reduce stress on the joints.

Regular Veterinary Check-ups

Schedule routine veterinary check-ups to assess joint health and identify any signs of hip or elbow dysplasia early on. Early detection allows for proactive management and treatment.

Early Detection and Prevention

Hip and elbow dysplasia are common concerns in large breeds like Newfoundlands. Regular veterinary check-ups and early detection are crucial. Implement preventive measures, including controlled growth through proper nutrition and maintaining a healthy weight.

Joint Supplements

Consider joint supplements, such as glucosamine and chondroitin, under the guidance of your veterinarian. These supplements support joint health and can be beneficial in managing conditions like dysplasia.

Heart and Eye Conditions

Cardiac Health

Newfoundlands are prone to certain heart conditions, including subaortic stenosis. Regular veterinary check-ups should include cardiac evaluations. Maintain a heart-healthy diet, and discuss any concerns or changes in behavior with your veterinarian promptly. Early detection allows for proactive management.

Eye Health

Regular eye examinations are essential for detecting potential conditions such as cataracts or progressive retinal atrophy. Keep their eyes clean and free from discharge, and seek immediate veterinary attention if you notice any abnormalities.

Maintaining a Healthy Weight

 Obesity can exacerbate certain health concerns, including those related to the heart and eyes. Regular exercise and a balanced diet contribute to maintaining a healthy weight.

Caring for your Newfoundland's nutrition and health requires a holistic approach that encompasses proper nutrition, preventive measures, and regular veterinary care. By choosing the right food, monitoring growth along with the concept of growing slow, are integral components of responsible ownership, and addressing common health concerns proactively, you contribute to the overall well-being and longevity of your beloved gentle giant. Regular collaboration with your veterinarian ensures a tailored health plan that meets the unique needs of your Newfoundland.

Chapter 9

Exercise and Enrichment - Keeping Your Newfoundland Happy and Healthy

Welcoming a Newfoundland into your life brings joy and companionship, but it also comes with the responsibility of meeting their unique exercise needs. In this chapter, we'll explore how to fulfill the physical and mental requirements of your gentle giant through a combination of land and water activities, interactive games, and strategies to prevent boredom and destructive behavior.

Meeting the Exercise Needs of a Newfoundland

Land and Water Activities

- **Land Exercises:** Newfoundlands may be large, but their exercise needs don't necessarily require intense workouts. Engage in low-impact land activities, such as moderate walks or short play sessions. Avoid strenuous exercise, particularly during their growth stages, to protect their developing joints. Due to their size, Newfoundlands benefit from moderate land exercises such as daily walks, hiking, and playtime in a secure backyard. Incorporate activities that cater to their natural instincts, like fetching or pulling light carts.
- **Water Activities:** Harness the Newfoundland's innate love for water by incorporating aquatic activities. These gentle giants are exceptional swimmers, and water exercises provide an excellent way to keep them fit without stressing their joints. Activities like swimming or supervised play in a shallow area are not only enjoyable for them but also beneficial for their overall well-being, promoting cardiovascular health and muscle strength.

Interactive Games for Mental Stimulation

Hide and Seek: Engage your Newfoundland's mind by playing hide and seek with treats or toys. This stimulates their problem-solving skills and enhances their bond with you.

Tug-of-War: This interactive game not only provides physical exercise but also mental stimulation. Ensure the game is played safely, using appropriate toys and maintaining control of the interaction.

Providing Puzzle Toys and Interactive Play

Puzzle Toys

Mental stimulation is equally crucial for your Newfoundland's well-rounded development. Introduce puzzle toys that challenge their problem-solving skills. Hide treats within puzzle toys or use interactive feeders to engage their minds during mealtime. Invest in puzzle toys that dispense treats as your Newfoundland solves them. This engages their cognitive abilities, providing mental stimulation and preventing boredom.

Interactive Play

Engage in interactive play, using toys that encourage problem-solving. Incorporate activities like fetch or agility exercises to keep them mentally and physically active.

Nose Work and Scent Games

Leverage their remarkable sense of smell with nose work activities. Hide treats or toys around the house or in the yard for them to find. This taps into their natural instincts, providing mental stimulation and a rewarding experience.

Variety in Toys

Keep a diverse range of toys to prevent monotony. Interactive toys, such as treat-dispensing balls or chew toys, can keep your Newfoundland engaged and entertained.

Rotate Toys

Rotate their toys regularly to keep them novel and exciting. This prevents boredom and ensures your Newfoundland remains interested in their playthings.

Obedience Training

Structured activities, such as obedience training, not only reinforce good behavior but also provide mental stimulation. Newfoundlands are intelligent and respond well to positive reinforcement. Regular training sessions provide mental stimulation and strengthen the bond between you and your Newfoundland. Incorporate commands into play and daily activities for a well-rounded approach.

Scheduled Play-dates

Arrange play-dates with other dogs to satisfy their social needs and provide additional mental and physical exercise. This also helps prevent loneliness and boredom.

Daily Walks

Incorporate daily walks into your routine. These outings serve as more than just exercise; they are opportunities for your Newfoundland to explore their environment, encounter new scents, and engage with the world around them.

Socialization Opportunities

Socialize your Newfoundland with various environments, people, and other dogs. Well-socialized dogs are more likely to be confident, adaptable, and less prone to anxiety or destructive behavior.

Conclusion

A happy and healthy Newfoundland is one that receives both physical and mental exercise essential for their physical health and mental well-being. A balanced approach, combining and incorporating a variety of land and water activities, interactive games, and structured play, you provide your gentle giant with the stimulation they need. Preventing boredom and destructive behavior is not just about physical activity but also about engaging their intelligent minds. This chapter explores diverse ways to keep your Newfoundland active, happy, and fulfilled, contributing to a harmonious and thriving relationship.

Chapter 10

Special Considerations for Senior Newfoundlands - Nurturing Your Aging Companion

As your beloved Newfoundland companion gracefully ages, their needs and requirements undergo a shift. This chapter explores the special considerations essential for providing optimal care to your senior Newfoundland, encompassing adjustments in nutrition, healthcare, exercise routines, and comfort measures.

Adjusting to the Aging Process

Senior Nutrition and Health Care

Tailored Diet

 Senior Newfoundlands, like their human counterparts, benefit from a diet tailored to their changing nutritional needs. Transition to a senior-specific dog food formulated to address issues such as joint health, maintaining a healthy weight, and supporting overall well-being. As Newfoundlands age, their nutritional needs may change and transitioning to a senior-specific diet is beneficial for their health and you should consult with your veterinarian to determine the most suitable dietary adjustments.

Weight Management

Obesity can exacerbate age-related health issues, particularly in large breeds like Newfoundlands. Monitor your senior Newfoundland's weight closely and adjust their diet as necessary to maintain a healthy body condition. Consult with your veterinarian to determine the ideal weight and nutritional requirements.

Regular Veterinary Check-ups

 Increase the frequency of veterinary check-ups to monitor your senior Newfoundland's health. This allows for early detection of age-related issues such as arthritis, dental problems, or organ function changes. Addressing these concerns promptly enhances their quality of life.

Modified Exercise Routines and Comfort Measures

Gentle Exercise

While exercise remains important for senior Newfoundlands,Adjust exercise routines to accommodate your senior Newfoundland's changing abilities. Shorter, more frequent walks and gentle activities like swimming can help maintain mobility without causing strain on aging joints.

Comfort Measures

 Enhance their living environment to accommodate their changing needs. Provide comfortable bedding and consider orthopedic options to support aging joints. Elevate food and water bowls to reduce strain on the neck and back. Ensure your senior Newfoundland has easy access to favorite resting spots, minimizing the need to climb or navigate stairs.

Joint Supplements

Introduce joint supplements, such as glucosamine and chondroitin, to support joint health. These supplements can contribute to improved mobility and comfort for senior Newfoundlands dealing with conditions like arthritis.

Conclusion

Navigating the senior years with your Newfoundland requires a blend of attentive care and thoughtful adjustments. As your Newfoundland companion enters their senior years, it's essential to adapt to their changing needs with love and care. This chapter delves into considerations for senior Newfoundlands, from adjusting their nutrition to modifying exercise routines and implementing comfort measures. By embracing these adjustments, you ensure that your aging gentle giant continues to lead a comfortable, happy, and dignified life, surrounded by the warmth and care they deserve.

In the forthcoming chapters, we'll delve into advanced aspects of senior care, explore techniques for enhancing their quality of life, and continue our journey through the nuanced care routines tailored to the evolving needs of your senior Newfoundland companion.

Chapter 11

Newfoundland Community and Activities - Building Connections and Making a Difference

This chapter explores the enriching aspects of engaging with the Newfoundland community and various activities. Whether through breed clubs, events, volunteering, or therapy work, these endeavors not only deepen your connection with the breed but also contribute to the greater well-being of Newfoundlands and the community at large. Embracing these opportunities allows you to share your love for the gentle giant while making a positive impact within the Newfoundland community.

Welcoming a Newfoundland into your life not only brings the joy of companionship but also opens doors to a vibrant community of fellow enthusiasts. This chapter explores the various ways you can engage with the Newfoundland community, from participating in breed clubs and events to volunteering and embracing therapy work with these gentle giants.

Engaging with the Newfoundland Community

Breed Clubs and Events - Finding Your Local Newfoundland Club

Joining a local Newfoundland breed club is an excellent way to connect with other Newfoundland enthusiasts with a wealth of information, support, opportunities to engage and share experiences, as well as stay updated on breed-specific events. These clubs often organize gatherings, play-dates, and informational sessions that can enhance your understanding of the breed.

National and International Events

Explore national and international Newfoundland-specific events, such as dog shows, competitions, meet-ups, or specialty events hosted by breed clubs. These gatherings not only provide an opportunity to showcase your Newfoundland's unique qualities but also offer a chance to learn from seasoned owners, breeders, and experts in the Newfoundland community. These gatherings provide a platform to learn more about the breed, share experiences, and build lasting connections with other Newfoundland enthusiasts.

Educational Seminars and Workshops

Many breed clubs host educational seminars and workshops covering a range of topics, from health and grooming to training and behavior. Participating in these events can deepen your knowledge and contribute to your Newfoundland's well-being.

Volunteering Opportunities

Explore volunteering opportunities within the Newfoundland community or at local animal shelters or visiting nursing homes, hospitals, or schools. The calming presence of a Newfoundland can bring joy to those in need. Participate in events that promote responsible dog ownership, rescue efforts, or community education. Volunteering not only contributes to the well-being of Newfoundlands but also strengthens the sense of community among owners.

Therapy Dog Certification

Consider engaging your Newfoundland in therapy work. Newfoundlands are renowned for their gentle and compassionate nature, making them excellent candidates for therapy work. Newfoundlands' gentle nature makes them well-suited for therapy visits to hospitals, nursing homes, or schools. Consider getting your Newfoundland certified as a therapy dog. Organizations like Therapy Dogs International (TDI) and Pet Partners offer certification programs. Completing these programs not only allows your Newfoundland to spread happiness and comfort but also fosters a deeper bond between you and your furry companion.

Search and Rescue Training

Leverage the Newfoundland's natural swimming abilities and strong work ethic by exploring search and rescue training programs. While this requires commitment and rigorous training, it taps into the breed's historical role as water rescue dogs. It's a fulfilling way to channel their energy into a purposeful and rewarding activity.

Networking and Support

Connecting with other Newfoundland owners provides a valuable network of support. Whether you're a first-time owner seeking advice or a seasoned enthusiast sharing your experiences, the Newfoundland community is a welcoming and supportive space.

Educational Opportunities

Breed clubs, events, and activities offer ongoing educational opportunities. Stay informed about the latest in Newfoundland health, grooming, training, and overall care. The collective knowledge within the community can be a valuable resource throughout your journey with your Newfoundland.

Strengthening the Bond with Your Newfoundland

Engaging in community activities not only benefits you but also strengthens the bond with your Newfoundland. Participating in events, volunteering, and exploring new activities together contribute to a shared sense of purpose and fulfillment.

Conclusion

The Newfoundland community is a vibrant and inclusive space where you can share your love for these gentle giants, learn from others, and contribute to the well-being of the breed. Whether it's participating in breed events, volunteering for therapy work, or engaging in search and rescue training, the Newfoundland community offers a plethora of activities that go beyond the conventional role of pet ownership.

As you explore these opportunities, you not only enrich your own life but also contribute to the collective welfare and appreciation of this remarkable breed. In the upcoming chapters, we'll delve into advanced aspects of Newfoundland care, explore techniques for enhancing their quality of life, and continue our journey through the nuanced care routines tailored to the evolving needs of your Newfoundland companion.

Chapter 12

Conclusion: Reflecting on the Journey with Your Newfoundland

As you embark on this remarkable journey with your Newfoundland, it's essential to take moments to reflect on the milestones and achievements you've celebrated together. This chapter has explored the ways in which you can engage with the Newfoundland community, expanding your connection beyond the four walls of your home. Now, let's delve into the significance of celebrating these moments and the enduring bond forged with your gentle giant.

Celebrating Milestones and Achievements

Growth and Development

Reflect on the journey from the early days of puppy-hood to the mature stages of your Newfoundland's life. Celebrate the growth and development they've undergone, marveling at the transformation from a playful pup to the majestic companion they've become.

Training Triumphs

Consider the training milestones you've achieved together. Whether it's mastering basic commands, conquering a challenging trick, or successfully navigating a training program, each accomplishment is a testament to your dedication and the intelligence of your Newfoundland.

Community Involvement

Take pride in the moments you've spent engaging with the Newfoundland community. Whether you've participated in breed events, volunteered for therapy work, or explored unique activities together, these experiences contribute to a rich tapestry of shared memories.

The Lifelong Bond with Your Gentle Giant

Unwavering Companionship

The bond forged with your Newfoundland is a testament to the unwavering companionship these gentle giants provide. Through thick and thin, your Newfoundland has been a source of comfort, joy, and unconditional love. Reflect on the countless moments where their presence made a difference in your life.

Shared Adventures

Consider the adventures you've embarked on together – from outdoor excursions to lazy days spent curled up on the couch. The shared experiences form the foundation of a unique relationship, one characterized by trust, loyalty, and an understanding that transcends words.

Lessons Learned

Cherish the lessons your Newfoundland has taught you. Their patience, resilience, and boundless affection offer insights into living in the present moment and finding joy in the simple pleasures of life. As you reflect on these lessons, you'll likely find that the bond you share goes beyond the roles of owner and pet.

In concluding this chapter, take a moment to appreciate the multifaceted journey you've embarked on with your Newfoundland. Celebrate the triumphs, both big and small, and recognize the profound impact your gentle giant has had on your life. The Newfoundland community serves as a supportive backdrop to this journey, providing a space for shared experiences, knowledge, and camaraderie.

As you reflect on the milestones, achievements, and the enduring bond with your Newfoundland, you'll likely discover that the journey is as enriching for you as it is for your gentle giant. In the upcoming chapters, we'll continue to explore advanced aspects of Newfoundland care, offering insights and guidance for the evolving needs of your beloved companion.

Newfoundland's endearing qualities become an integral part of your everyday life, and the shared memories form the foundation of a relationship that brings immeasurable joy and fulfillment. As you continue this odyssey with your Newfoundland, the shared experiences become threads in the rich tapestry of a lifelong companionship, embodying the true essence of the human-canine bond.

As you reflect on the journey with your Newfoundland, the immense bond forged between you and your gentle giant becomes a testament to the joys and challenges of canine companionship. From the early days of navigating puppy-hood to the mature and steadfast presence they've become, the journey is a mix of shared moments, both heartwarming and humorous. The resilience, loyalty, and unwavering love your Newfoundland exudes create an undeniable connection that transcends the roles of owner and pet. Celebrating milestones and weathering challenges together